AF338266

EL RIO

EL RIO

Steven P. Klepeis

RESOURCE *Publications* · Eugene, Oregon

EL RIO

Resource Publications
An Imprint of Wipf and Stock Publishers
199 W. 8th Ave., Suite 3
Eugene, OR 97401

www.wipfandstock.com

PAPERBACK ISBN: 978-1-6667-8189-2
HARDCOVER ISBN: 978-1-6667-8190-8
EBOOK ISBN: 978-1-6667-8191-5

VERSION NUMBER 061423

CONTENTS

RIVERS

1

In the centuries of farmers' sons
who have gone down the hill
to the insect laden rust brown
mud banks, and white fluffs of

cottonwood seed on black
backwaters, I have been
one. In centuries of summers
and the smell of sweet corn

under the long days
of an unimaginable sun, I
have cast for and sought
the redolence of fresh rivers,

and their fish, landed
in their milk slime
protections against parasites.
With only my skin and bones,

and blood to protect me,
I was immersed in the
microscopic richness of unfiltered
mountain streams, lifted

in moving mountain air, with
heat of June and taint of January,
in sudden soul awakening cold rains.
Families upstream bathing.

2

Rivers flow in young men,
in all their strength,
mustered up in dawn mornings
from country births,

and carry all that they
collect in growing, the
soul's wooden impediments,
the flash of hard rain.

Upstream far enough, just below
glaciers living and dead,
few hands take from
the high tributaries

or stand the tumble of flash floods.
And yet, after seeps and puddles, ponds,
lakes, reservoirs, swamps and estuaries,
down on the beaches and

flats of sacred rivers,
young and old find
strength in heart and soul
to love and bathe in

humanities of rivers,
the long flow.

EL RIO

1

The Rio, moonless
obsidian, flowing in
ambient starlight, not a
single random splash.

Basalt walls black,
the Miocene flow
in the old rift five
million years ago, cut

sharp by the little stream
that from the beginning
of the Holocene joined
the four basins

into a river, the
eventual weight
of ice water
first an eroding

trickle, then
an explosion, a
plowing, gouging flood.
Boulders, soil,

trees, gravel and mud.
How tame now the
August night here,
insect quiet, feeling

my way along silicate
exfoliations in
granite.

2

Pitch black. Felt
like a swarm of black
around my head, my hands,
my invisible feet.

Scree-sliding the
blindness down five,
eight, maybe twelve feet
at a time, to abrupt

stops at frost-broken
boulders. Finally,
water, and the
dimmest gleam of

polished waves of
rocks, more felt than seen,
Colorado's New Mexican
sediments at waterline.

The warm air, above, under
the Venus crescent, now
four hundred feet down,
cooled by water's lessons.

3

At first, silence.
But then, a leaking
current and seep
where soil forms the shore.

Carrying the essential
eight-footer, in waders,
caddis elk wing on the line,
parachute flies, Trico spinners

pinned to my vest,
above my dangling net
and chain I wade a blind
right foot out along

the stony bottom
of drowned boulders,
as if entering an offset room
deep down a mineshaft,

past hope of surface light.
And the current, God's
weight, pressing every
inch of hips, and legs

and feet backward.
Counting steps sideward.
Ears casting timing and intensity,
the trickling measure of shore.

I am cast off,
body the first boat.
Water its dangerous
trust.

4

Balance. Balance.
Bump of rubber,
slide-up of toes
inside, rapid cold,

stiffness in legs,
hips, spreading.
A soldier's body
in the Argonne.

Neanderthal legs
wrapped tight in bear skins,
mammoth fur cloak
over the hungry torso,

wading ice melt.
I am cast off.
I have left the waking,
walking worlds,

my double absence,
the one I am from
and the one I live in,
to enter double presence,

conscious and
unconscious,
simultaneous,
existence

only, with treasures
of brown trout
lurking about in eddies
and backwaters.

5

Arms up for
balance, swing about
left, about right, taking
my top weight.

No definition
of location in
this movement now,
and place known only as

the natural ruins of
former worlds, colossal,
and rendered parts
and bits. The living

and the dead lie
around me together
in their silent dark,
and suddenly down

and deeper, to the brim
of chest waders, and
a foot-search for higher
ground in the river bed.

Now I must be midstream
as the three middle
fingertips can feel the
convergence of flows

around the cabin-sized
boulder I know from
daylight is there, and
I work out ready my pole.

6

From its two-handed role
as balance beam, to my right
half-clasping the reel
and grip, and my

left in seventh octave
delicacy upon the loop
of line, and dripping icy water,
the two hands together,

like raising a conductor's
wand, to two o'clock,
to ten o'clock, to two
o'clock, to ten o'clock,

the right hand's power
in the whip of the wrist,
the left fingers' synchronous
anchoring, then tendering

the reel's line, to
reach that upstream
void, that exact spot,
seeing only the line

up in the air under
starlight, that one,
just one, with dark iris
ringed by amber, might

spot the fall and
rapid float of the
dry fly, and strike
the subconscious.

7

And from within
the dark mysteries
of fresh water
Pleistocene, a white-

ness at the gills, white
lining of the vicelike mouth,
the upper vomerines,
and canines sharp, body

one muscle of hunger,
flexed upon the fly
so hard, it almost burned
my fingertips and stole the rod.

The whiteness flash in
pitch blackness nearly
impossible to see,
but instantly both hands

anchored and pulled
and pulled, and the left
started pulling in line,
and right worked the tension

of the set hook. A predator's
style of fight, full of
leap and slap, and splash
of star silver water

under his own galaxy.
There was no thought.
Under my steady eyes,
I grew warm.

THE RONDOUT

1

From way up near
the southeast base
of the rocky col between
Rocky Mountain and
Balsam Cap, collecting the
springs of the plateaus'
eroding rock sieves,
it falls into the open,
in high air, in pure,
pre-carbon, bubbling
and blathering oxygen
and nitrogen,
in its first breath.

Ice age spillway of a
prehistoric lake that
once lay aloft.
Now, only a little way down,
and by the time it reaches
Picket Brook, it has
ripped out sandstone
voids, and washed open
holes for the homes
of trout. This high and
narrow, no one has
ever seen or caught
anything but brookies here.

Little from big, high
in the watershed, brookies
are the only ones who can
make it up this far.
How many times I
hiked up there,
April 1st, still eight
inches of snow,
and with butter
and almonds, salt,
pepper and cast iron
skillet, cooked and ate
half the caught limit.

2

The State now says that
above the Sundown Creek
confluence, the Rondout
will not be stocked.
Thankfully, they list it
as Wild-Quality.
Thankfully, only those
with the hunger will there
fish. From there down
extends the human
competition, with State signs
paltering, "This is your
drinking water."

And there the State dumps
tons of brown trout, crowd
pleasers, who like the lebensraum,
where the creek slows
and widens, and a
minority of rainbows
give up their own
habitats and move
upstream to a faster,
colder flow and slimmer
bank-full width. The two
do not interbreed, and
the ecology is "natural."

But I would still go
above Stone Cabin
Brook, Bear Hole
Brook, and turn north
before Peekamoose
Lake, without trails,
as far as
the brookies go.
Beyond that, the
mountains own
you, all of you,
where soul is body,
and breath is hunger.

3

Coal. 1828-99. New York.
They knew where.
They knew how immigrant
work would build a waterway,
a canal, from Honesdale,
PA, to the wide Hudson
and the quaff of NYC.
Hunger, before breath.
Anthracite, the best.
The 1825 Wall Street
crowd oversubscribed.
Open October, 1828.
90,000 tons in 1832.

1950's Rosendale, ex
canal town, in a mile
of Main Street, had
fifteen bars. The waft
of tavern keepers in
St. Peter's church on
Sundays. Drained in 1898,
the lost jobs chased
down a bottle, a
tradition sustained by
lost lives and wars.
Coykendall kept
Rosendale to Rondout

active to supply
Rosendale Cement
out to the Hudson,
down to the grids
of empire. That
began years before, then with
James McEntee and JA Roebling
and the East River Bridge,
Brooklyn, footings of
Rosendale quarried
cement. Immigrant lives
lost in the caisson depths
and the bends.

4

Loss, measured against
gain, is Olber's Paradox,
success the receding light,
seen, maybe, or not,
a sky mostly black, the
reward only of fact, which
ignorance worries
to death. But in the real
world where nothing is except
the living and the self,
there is enough light
and dark, enough
sight.

Hudson's third,
sailing for the Dutch,
saw the mouth of
the Rondout and the fires
of the Munsees, and
Mohicans north and west, up
in the (later) Catskill Mountains.
The Dutch, following
Hudson's notes, found it,
and named it.
The rest, as they say,
is blood on the altar
of Babel,

which the winners call
history. Esopus, all
from the Hudson west
and southwest, over the
Catskills and Nicolaes
Visscher I's 1656 map,
to the Delaware and
the Lenni Lenape, the
original people. Upstream,
just shy of eight miles and
98 feet of elevation, over
the bouldered sands and
bedrock shales brought

from eroded glaciation,
they found a series of
rapids, of no special note,
which they called a falls,
later named for Lefever,
but no blacksmith ever
hammered here. I, from
eight to eighteen years,
hammered however the
summer's low-water holes
of largemouth bass, and
sunnies and crappies and
smallmouth bass, and

downstream, catfish and eels.
Before that, we bathed there,
to drown the dog days
of August and the insidious
irritations of working
poverty, the back sweat of
dirt laboring skin. It was where
my father on his right
shoulder carried me over
foot-deep cobbled waters.
It was where for me
nature began to hold
also people.

MOMBACCUS CREEK

1

Water is the way,
through eons, across
Devonian bedrock
scraped bare by
one point five miles of ice,
torrent melts
and runoffs, spillways,
streams and river
valleys carved out.
The rolling rise and
fracture under my feet.
Roll, pitch and yaw of
steel on tires, on
Holocene streets.
Samsonville Road
to Mombaccus Creek.

2

The king stream
of posted land
and brookies. At
dawn, working upstream,
from the road, west,
sun behind, thick,
close canopy, water
all a long plain blackness,
pimpled into currents
toward eyes that cannot see
trout in six inch flows.
Pure trust, to cast
those dark flats and flows.
To reach out into
my own
invisible shadow.

3

Too close in here for
fly rod length, so
my short six footer
and light spinner
swings easily, my
Shakespeare, articulate
in small places.
At first, I doubt
the shallow water;
their every eye's peripherals
are constantly in focus,
cones tuned to the spectrum,
rods that see through darkness.

4

Selection has made us
a fair match. A dry fly
in this swiftness needs
only a B weight to get
the monofilament out
twenty feet. First cast
perfect. The bail tripped
before my Prince Nymph
sinks. But no hit. In
seven more casts, no
hits. It is early morning;
it is May; it is small
water, late spring depth.

5

Now my doubts
invade this. Three hundred
yards further, landowners
own and have closed the
stream. That will be
enough to tell me
if they are still here,
in these cold water
puddles and pools.
Just beyond these
bordering trees, the
planted field's soil
bursts in sunlight.

6

And the flat current
explodes, splashed up
with my line, a fish
in air,
dim in diamonds,
as if not caught, but
caught, and screeching
drag in the reel.
And now I am the clear
line that connects me
to it. Now I am
the hand on the
scooping net.

7

The hand that
runs the chain link past
the bright red gills
and out the rounded
mouth, removes the fly.
An eight inch fully adult
male, kyped, a pale orange on
white belly, yellow stipple
throughout dark olive dorsal skin.
Renoir's Venetian reds
a brushed touch to each
under-fin. And I am
caught in the wide eyes.

THE PECOS

1

Ice the son, gravity
the mother. They came
out of eternity,
banging the earth
into mysteries.
Precambrian orogeny, erosion.
Gravity, the gatherer,
gas and dust pulled

into the heat
of her molten core.
Then ice, born
of her cold wobble,
comes, the finisher,
grinding the crust to rubble
released in outwash every
twenty-six thousand years.

Nearly 3 billion years
are veiled by the rocks'
unconformities, appearing
where they shouldn't appear,
absent where they should.
High in the Cowles-Ribera
sub-basin, where the river
is untouched, and every minute

free, I spend my thoughts
and footsteps among its
insects and trees,
and metamorphic boulders
dislodged from
foundations of time
by the second uplifts, the
Laramide Orogeny.

2

Geologic time defies
the traveling mind's
consciousness. The first,
ancestral Rockies arose
during Pennsylvanian time.
Colorado and New Mexico
were near the equator then,
when Laurentia started to move.

The fault-bounded basins
were filled with shallow water.
In seventy million years of
erosion, it was all gone, down
to the bottoms of warm inland seas.
Precambrian gneiss from the dawn
of earth, heaved upon the younger
sea sediments, in Laramide uplifts.

The mother and son of Earth
take what never belonged to us,
and give it back differently.
Our shells and bones buried,
are carried far from their souls,
who, perhaps, as these, flit about
as food, for the ceaseless hunger
above and within ceaseless water.

It begins, high, rain or snow,
where waters have no names,
in seeps above tributaries,
above spawning beds, fresh,
purified through gravels,
sands and clays
left there by ice,
ten thousand years ago.

3

Pure, for the insects and fish.
Pure for the animals who
must drink here, jack rabbits
and moles, big headed
clumsy elk. Pure, to feed
the roots of asters, balloon
flowers, dwarf clovers, dandelions
enough for all wishes.

Pure, to be sought
by trout, and warm enough,
late May through July,
delectable tan caddis,
pale morning duns, golden
stoneflies, yellow sallies,
red quills, tricos, the sun's
gift, pure, and caught

in rotation, as the axis leans,
rotation's millings
into the consequence of life,
warmth and birth, hunger
of all earth. Distant gases
cooling into carbon. Cell
to cell upon cell, water
and air, green earth.

4

Geology makes no apology,
nor do I. It is the most pieces
of the whole story,
all the elements, dirt,
air and water. It is who
and what we have come
from, and been and are,
and might be.

It is curious that
the fish we call cutthroat
is the one with the cut
throat appearance, so to
speak, but nonetheless, fierce
as any in their fight, or
so they say, as I have
never caught any, nor fat

browns, rainbows,
or cutbows in the
Pecos, not for lack
of trying. Down steep slopes
from Highway 63, strewn
with ponderosas, and higher,
bristlecones and limbers
patient of slow time,

and droughts, and the
comedy of fishermen,
and sliding boulders.
Down only the first
vignette in waders.
Working farther upstream,
the valley sharpens the V.
Back up is murder.

THE COLDWATER

1

Unaware, we chose
Sunday, of course, the
people's day for God
and baptisms in the
river, and prayers that
we all go to glory,
some day. In the shaded seclusion
of its headwater, where cold
springs surface quietly all about
in rings of ripples, we
were dropped off and,
tubes in hand, had almost
shoved off into the
West Fork, Big Coldwater
Creek, when the yellow
school bus pulled up,
and parked on the little pull-off
before the culvert crossing.

A First Baptist Church,
but couldn't see which.
In a habit of speaking
silently, our stillness focused.
Worshipers, in Sunday clothes,
and then the blessed, in
white, walked with a pastor
into the dark water. We
froze, sequestered in brush.
Delicately, taking their hands
in firm belief, he
relaxed them backward
and retrieved the joyous
faces full of water,
graced in spotty sunlight.

To see that was to share it
in heartbeats, and to know
that our irreligious selves
would not forget it.
Minutes vanished in the
songs of cicadas, and in
the fluff of air of
birds wings moving through
the morning. It was not
long, but all, maybe
twelve, were set fast
in God's grace, and
quick as they came, left.
And without a word,
we pushed off.

2

The West Fork just
appears, in the panhandle's
pine forests, in what
seems an excavated
channel or canal,
but only a quarter mile,
maybe three feet deep,
probably just a temporary
place to hold cut logs.
But it ends, abruptly,
where the clay shelf
it sits on drops,
and the entire flow
becomes a swamp.
Tubing the mild
current and following
whatever seemed
downstream, we
entered the sudden
coolness, darkness.

Loaded with tall cypress
that my submerged self
could feel, invisibly,
under black watery muck.
The subsurface flaring
of the cypress trunks
became our only solid
push-offs. No one swims
a swamp. It was a perfect
place, found but left
alone, in the timber rich
deep South. Full body,
up to the neck, suspended
in the rich organic slush,
with clear water, displaced,
that ran steadily three
inches over the top of it.
Awareness peaked.
Not a frog or snake seen,
but close, sensed
in the cautions of egrets.

It was probably only
a half mile, now that I
think back of the time
it took. Separated out
of earshot, unknown
how far but with little
thought of it in a mind
possessed by the sharp
instants of sense. Nothing
modern in here, except the
odd smell of the rubber
tube against the aroma
of watery earth and the trees
of Neolithic dreams.

Suddenly, a droning,
then weight of falling
water, then lowly a
dull roar, and splashing.
A waterfall of eight
feet, from the edge of the
clay and swamp down
into the full flowing stream.
A shout, close enough
to hear across gravity's
seam. Tubed down it,
nature's waterslide,
into thankful splashes,
and we were off
again, duck paddling
down the pure, quiet
stream.

3

Now the Florida August
sun conjured the soft
lyrics of all Southern
waters to rise in
the sweetness of orange
jasmine, like us,
escaping cultivation.
But invasive and
barring exploration
over the banks. We
moved within the
katydids emerging
from morning, who
were muted by the
high rasps of cicadas.

Within momentary absences
of those, and with no
wind and only the still air
heating above the water
and all through the trees,
another, summer sound
rose inside to the roof
of the skull, in the warmth
of the waking dream.
Startled by the message
of a hand reaching
down in the cold water
to paddle. The instant
evaporation of splashes
on hot rubber.
The immensity of the heat.

After miles of
floating slowly in
a dream, our
meandering took more
bends and shaded
curves through overhangs
and, current colder,
we flumed under
live oaks, buckeyes
and hornbeams, past
the undercut banks
of hardpan capped with
sand.

And after a series
of those, now about
three-quarters of
the trip, we beached
on a hot sandbar
and sat up in the
shade of the bank
the sun hadn't found
yet. Where a hundred
years meant nothing.
Where coarse gravel
kept the hourglass.
Outside this time,
virgin timber fell,
and oil plumed over
coal and steam.

But suddenly in that
barefoot, insect singing
air, a light bump of metal.
And then a boy's
laughter, upstream,
and no one yet in
sight. More bumps,
light in echoes. Two
voices, alarmed, then
laughing again, when
finally around the bend,
the boys, in jeans
hacked off at the knees,
bare chests and straw hats,
came manning the flow
in an old mason's tub,
with a coal shovel.

THE SANTA CRUZ

In the verdant
Cundiyo valley, in
open fields, past
old, abandoned
ranchitos, Medio Rio
and Frijoles Rio meet
at NM 503, the
Cundiyo Road,
and form the
Santa Cruz River.

All little more than
spring fed brooks
that have flowed here
in this carved valley
for countless years.
The rainbows stocked in
the Santa Cruz Reservoir
just a mile and a half
downstream have a
hard time coming up in

the low water
to spawn, and mostly
just stay in the lake.
Good to know.
The little pull-off
and canyon slope footpath
hemmed in and
surrounded by the
coyote willow wilderness
of hot dry July.

The entrance to the path
invisible. The ten foot
Santa Cruz completely
overgrown. No room
to wade the stream
and cast. No access
from the banks. The
fish and flies left to themselves.
The green walls sustained
by the under bank seeps.

Not a drop elsewhere
in the steep canyon walls,
in all the eroded, strewn
rubble of hills. Water
is taken for granted here. All
the upstream pastures
a miracle only of
cow manure.
Sierra Mosca is nature's
only patron of these streams.

Back to the car
after ass-busting forays,
my resolve was not
greater than the
patience of thick brush
and, if any, the quiet fish.
With five bucks of honesty
into the tin box, you can
park and fish the reservoir.
Good to know.

A parting note,
however, in
respect of balance,
coyote willow
helped to sustain
the Pueblos, in water jugs,
cradles, hats, bowls,
trays, baskets, seed
beaters, springtime inner
bark for rope. Prayer sticks.

www.ingramcontent.com/pod-product-compliance
Lightning Source LLC
Chambersburg PA
CBHW070735030726

47601CB00001B/30